The Art of the Fart

The Art of the Fart

Steve Bryant

SALAMANDER

Produced in 2008 by
Salamander Books
10 Southcombe Street
London W14 0RA

An imprint of Anova Books Company Ltd

This edition published 2005
Distributed in the U.S. and Canada by:
Sterling Publishing Co., Inc.
387 Park Avenue South
New York, NY 10016

10 9 8 7 6 5 4 3

ISBN 978 1 85648 732 0

Printed in China

Dedication

It is traditional at this point to thank the editor for his or her unfailing support throughout the enterprise. However, as I am an honest man, I feel it only fair to point out that the "gentleman" in question has resolutely failed to take me out for lunch, refused to buy me even a solitary drink, and lastly (and to my mind most heinously) overruled my truly inspired idea to release this book in a scratch and sniff format. So, no thanks required there. Instead this book is dedicated to Andrea for "lighting the way" on numerous occasions.

Picture credits

All Images are from the Anova Image Library except the following:

Corbis /Bettmann 41, 43, 61, 72, 125. / Hulton-Deutsch Collection 71. /John Springer Collection 62, 68. /Underwood & Underwood 79.

Jacket Images are from the Anova Image Library

Contents

Introduction 6
Fartasaurus 8
The Beau-Fart Scale 18
Farter Know Thyself 24
When and Where 36
Where To Fart 38
Where Not to Fart 48
Farting In History 66
The Path of the Third Eye 84
The Apprentice Farter 92
The Professional Farter 98
Master of Farts 102
Grand Master of Farts 106
Real Life Farting Heroes 112
Top Tens 120
Contents of the Average Fart 126

Introduction

Why do we fart? I'm not going to bore you with the scientific and biological facts of the matter because the bottom line is that we fart because it's funny. If you find yourself disagreeing with this statement in even the smallest way, you should put this book down now, ask yourself why you even picked it up in the first place, and go forth to begin the search for your long lost sense of humor.

Those of you who, wisely I might add, choose to continue with the flatulent odyssey set out before you will find within the following pages a treasure trove of trumping delights. You will have revealed to you matters of farting etiquette, the true part that farting and farters have played in the shaping of the world we live in, and an insight into the sacred order of The Path of the Third Eye. Various visual images will also be provided for your humorous delight.

I shall leave you with the thought that although I have chosen to keep this introduction short, it generally pays to be as long-winded as possible.

Fart long, fart loud, and, above all, fart proud.

"I fart therefore I am"

Descartes

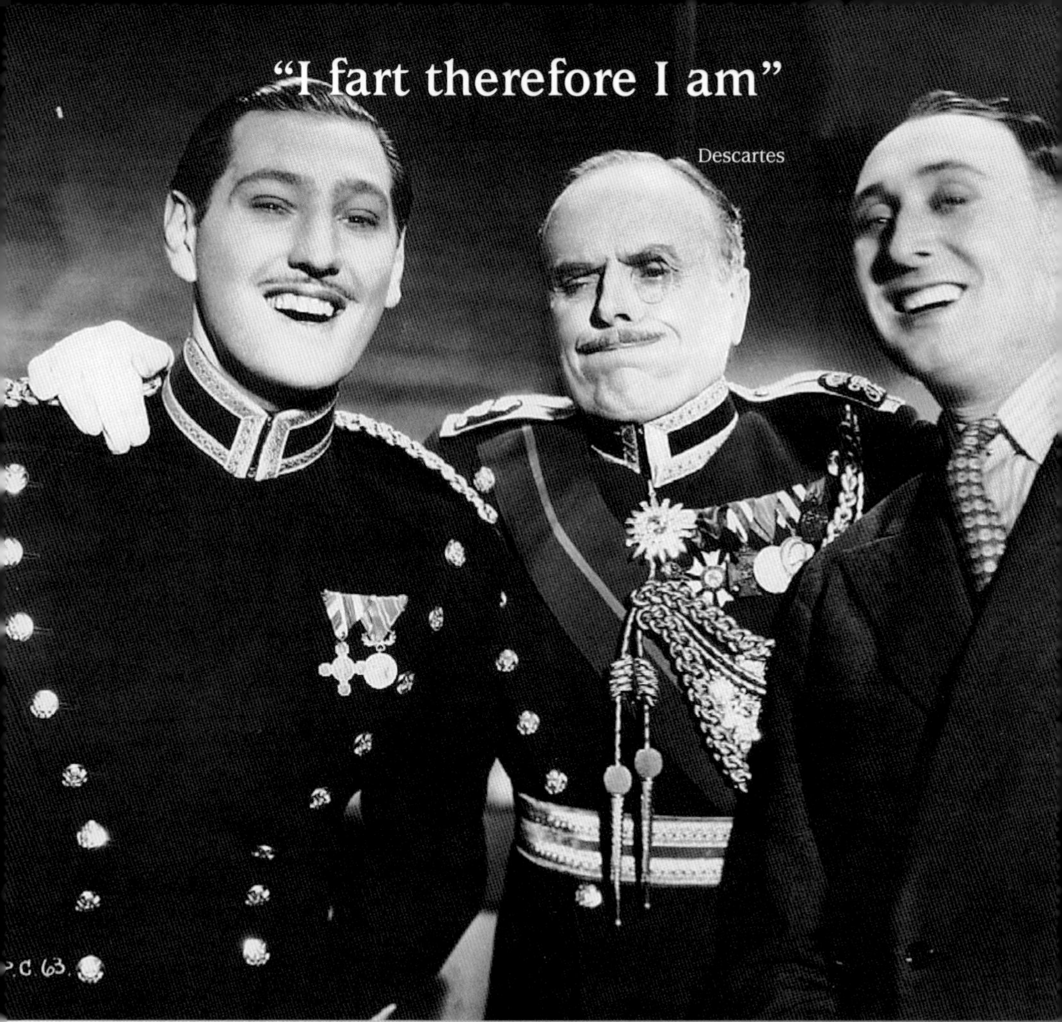

P.C. 63.

Fartasaurus (Types of Fart)

Before we go any further, it is important to have a working knowledge of the various farts at your disposal. There now follows a brief description of some of the most common types of flatulence available to both the amateur and professional purveyor of parps.

Ripper

Truly loud and long fart, think of a stuck bison bellowing in pain, but odor free. Blasts its way out so harshly that the farter may well be led to believe that their butt has been shredded in the process of letting it go. This is rarely the case but it is good to check.

Ripsnorter

The stench-laden sibling to the above. As loud as the Ripper but accompanied by a truly obnoxious smell. Will cause everyone in its vicinity to snort (and quite possibly gag) as their nostrils are assailed by a smell so foul that not even the owner can bear it.

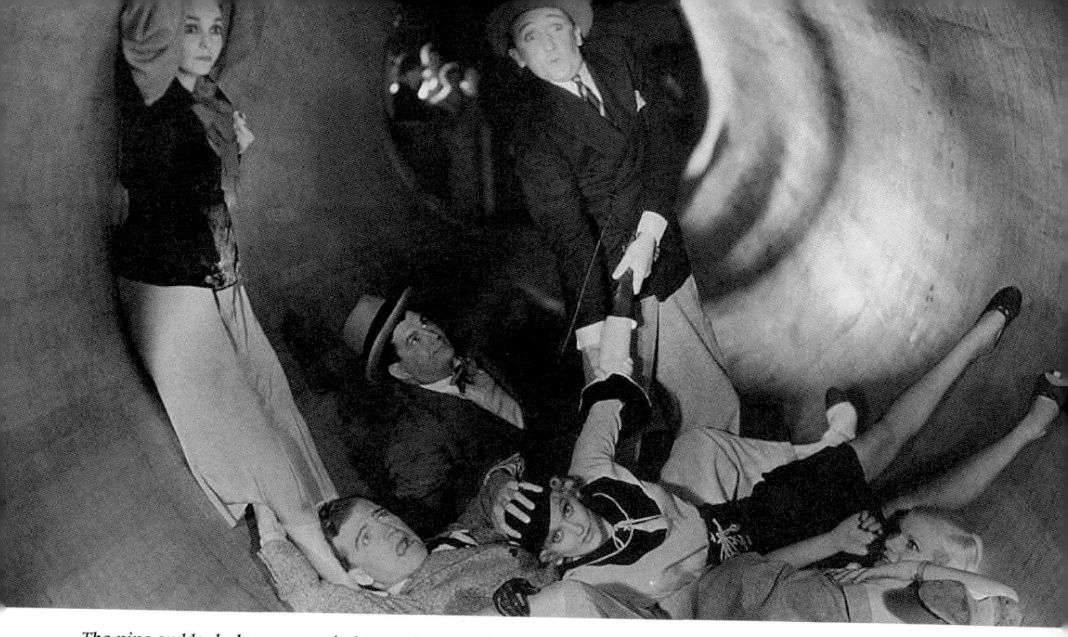

The pipe suddenly became a wind tunnel, when George let out a Ripper that really bowled them over.

Long Drawn Out Affair

A more gentle and drawn out but just as malodorous version of the Ripsnorter. In its typical form this fart is characterized by its noise—like a very small motorcycle—and the feeling that a gnome is blowing a raspberry out of your behind. Seconds after it is out, you'll be left in no doubt that your bottom has seriously misbehaved.

"Darn it," thought Jill. "I've only just had this chaise longue professionally dry-cleaned."

Cheeky One

The little beauty that just pops out without warning. It's a common enough fart but at the wrong time can lead to varying levels of embarrassment. The only saving grace in these situations is that it probably won't be much of a stinker.

P.O.S.H.H. Fart

Oh dear, oh dear, oh dear. It's a Cheeky One gone horribly wrong. As with the Cheeky One you will have no warning, not even the faintest pre-fart tremor—but the important difference here is that this devil will Pop Out and Stink to High Heaven. Pray that when it does sneak up on you, you are not only alone, but also in a wide-open space with plenty of room for diffusion.

Squeaker

You know the scene. A pair of young lovers have got lost in some dark, forbidding woods. Having walked for hours they finally reach human habitation. This, of course, is an equally dark and forbidding mansion. Just as they reach the top of the steps and are about to knock on the ornate brass door-knocker, the doors slowly creak open. This is the sound made by a squeaker. You won't know if it's going to smell until it's out there. Always a gamble this one.

Wet One

Not good. Usually only happens in early childhood or after extreme overindulgence in alcohol—in either case when muscle control is not all it could be. Will generally just pop out with no prior warning. The farter will for a brief, blissful moment believe that no real harm has been done. However, an unnervingly warm moistness in the rear-pant area will soon give the lie to this thought. Time to find the nearest toilet facility, remove the offending soiled underwear, and start the mop-up operation. Discreet disposal of the underwear is tricky but an absolute must: you're going commando until you can get home for a change of underwear. If you are both sober and over the age of ten and still dropping wet ones, hang your head in shame. Go home and work on your muscle control.

Follow Through

To be avoided at all costs. This is the same as a wet one but we're talking solids rather than mere moistness here. This author has only met one person prepared to admit to an adult follow-through episode. The story involved an almost-Herculean consumption of alcohol, a crowded

Jean began to notice that whenever she met Don, a motorcycle would backfire in the street outside.

rush-hour train carriage, and absolutely no control whatsoever. In short, the carriage emptied at the next stop and a mop-up operation involving a newspaper ensued. Turns out that newspapers really aren't that absorbent at all. If this should ever happen to you, my advice would be to tell absolutely no one. If there are witnesses who can't be bribed, then emigrate—you will NEVER live this down.

When the judge ordered, "Silence in court," Arthur's bottom was guilty of immediate contempt.

Silent But Violent (also known as Silent But Deadly)

The stealth weapon in the farter's armory. This little puppy will make no noise at all on the way out, but it won't be long until everyone in the room knows that someone has let rip. Has been known to clear a crowded space in seconds flat. People will suspect that something has crawled up your passage and died such is the unnaturally gruesome stench. The only question left is whether or not you want to own up to your emission. Probably not.

Flapper

Another drawn out fart. This one slowly eases its way out and takes its time doing it. Sounds as if your cheeks are gently flapping in the breeze. Generally not too much of a stinker.

Stinger or Ring Stinger

This is the curry or chili-fueled cousin of the squeaker. Will leave you with a behind that feels like it's been dragged across a cheese grater. Always stinks.

Stalker

This is the one that catches you out when you know you've got a fart that needs to be freed, just not in the present company. You thoughtfully leave the room and let rip out of earshot. Having let a suitable time elapse, you saunter nonchalantly back in to the room thinking that you've got away with it, only to find that the stench has remained around you like some kind of malodorous cloak.

Short, Sharp Shocker

Rings out like a gunshot and bursts out with no warning. You'll be as stunned by this little beauty as everyone within earshot. It is basically a condensed Ripper—a good five to ten seconds worth of wind, and its associated loudness, contained in a one- or two-second burst.

Double-Barreled

A fart of two halves if you will. One for the connoisseur this, as for full effect a great deal of control is required. Remember when you were a child and you used to skim stones across the water? Well, this is the farting equivalent. A staccato fart that has more than one distinct

Old Howie's violent Shocker was the inspiration for the modern day ejector seat.

"movement," the more syllables you can give this the better. Definitely a case of the more the merrier.

The Beau-Fart Scale

In the early 1760s, a method was devised to measure the force of farts. Jeremiah Trump, a keen farter of Yorkshire, England, decided to rate the efforts of his and his friends' bowels utilizing a scale of measurement which he referred to as "Yee Goode Farte Scale." Several of his friends, being of a somewhat pretentious nature, insisted that the scale would have greater public acceptance and popularity if it were to be named in a faux-foreign manner and thus the "Beau-Fart Scale" was born. A translation into modern English is provided in this section.

To escape his wife's constant farting, Chester sought refuge in the street.

The Beau-Fart Scale

Force	Description	Specifications of Flatulence Within Pants/Skirts
0	Calm	All is calm, no rear-end action whatsoever.
1	Light Air	Minor chuff, a light warmness may be felt. No disturbance of underwear. Noise levels negligible.
2	Light Breeze	Wind felt on underwear, loose garments may rustle in the breeze. Sound vaguely audible to purveyor of wind.
3	Gentle Breeze	Underwear in definite motion. In quiet room farter will hear the fruit of his/her labors.
4	Moderate Breeze	Raises eyebrows, those in close attendance fully aware that fart has occurred.
5	Fresh Breeze	Short skirts lightly lifted, underwear visibly ruffled. Small animals strangely disturbed.
6	Strong Breeze	Underwear elastic stretched, this'll blow your skirt up and no mistake. Audible above normal conversation.
7	Near Gale	Bottom stretched, underwear strained. You are the center of attention even in a crowded room. Heavy odor more than likely.
8	Gale	Panty elastic snaps under strain, sore bottom likely. Stench inevitable. Social exclusion a distinct possibility.

Force	Description	Specifications of Flatulence Within Pants/Skirts
9	Severe Gale	Belts and braces may well buckle under the strain. Possible corrosion of the septum. Audible in adjacent rooms.
10	Storm	Possible destruction of underwear. Long-term damage to nasal cavity inevitable. Can be heard in surrounding buildings. Outside foliage disturbed.
11	Violent Storm	Foliage flattened, small trees bent. Poorly constructed buildings in danger of structural damage. Clothing unlikely to remain attached.
12	Hurricane	Underwear shredded, pants wrecked, skirts blown to neck level, and emergency services alerted (probably no need to call them, anyone within a five-mile radius who has not been deafened/nasally stunned will be more than aware of what has occurred). Paramedics required immediately.

Author's note: While they were featured in Trump's original scale and are thus included, there are no medically, or otherwise, recorded human occurrences of either Violent Storm- or Hurricane-level fart activity. It is possible that like volcanoes, such incidents occur only every millennium.

One day Marlon Brando, no fan of the French, was introduced to the daughter-in-law of a senior French government official. Rather than rise from his spot on the sofa, Brando offered the woman his finger, commanding her to pull (*Tirez*). When the woman obliged, Brando unleashed what one observer later described as a "Wagnerian fart"...

"Mitzi, lieblings, you didn't have a second helping of Frau Blucher's sauerkruat, did you...?"

"Blow winds, and crack your cheeks!"

William Shakespeare, *King Lear*

Farter Know Thyself

What Kind of Farter are You?

We all fart, that's just a fact of nature and the vast majority of the human race just gets on with it. Chances are though that if you've got a copy of this book in your hands, you have a more than passing interest in the passing of wind. Either that or it was a present from a) a friend or acquaintance with a love of the fine art or b) an older relative who wants to be thought of as cool (or who just couldn't think of anything else to get you).

Assuming that you do have a personal interest, you will more than likely fall into one of the categories listed in this section.

Within five miles of setting off, Mary's traveling companions had voted that she transfer to second class.

Loud and Proud

The true extrovert of the farting world. Loves to fart and takes a genuine pride in his art, it doesn't matter where or when. Generally speaking the loud and proud farter is male, though there are some rare females of the species. The louder and smellier the fart, the better. Prospective partners of the Loud and Proud farter should beware—farting under the duvet and then holding you under the covers so that you can fully appreciate the fruitiness of their labors is considered an act of love.

Favored Fart: Loves all kinds of farts but has a particular penchant for the Ripsnorter. The obvious exceptions to this rule are the Wet One and Follow Through—not even a Loud and Proud farter wants to be associated with these acts of social suicide. Will always own up with great pride to a Silent But Violent.

Brunhilda's uncanny ability to let one rip on the hour, every hour, made her the toast of the timekeepers' convention.

REAL COCKTAILS

Little Maisie's stitching lessons were never pleasant after Auntie Doreen dropped one.

Shy and Retiring

By far the most common female farter. There's no avoiding the fact that we all fart, it's just that in the ideal world of the Shy and Retiring farter it would never happen, let alone in public. The complete opposite of the Loud and Proud farter.

Favored Fart: Absolutely none as a preference, but a gentle Flapper in the privacy of their own privy if they must.

Sly and Retiring

The Sly and Retiring farter would like you to believe that they never let one go. This is of course a lie, what they truly love is to let one rip and lay the blame on someone else in the room. The sly and retiring farter will always be the first to offer the "he who smelt it must have dealt it" excuse.

Favored Fart: There can be only one, the Silent but Violent is the stock in trade of this sly devil.

Pyromaniac

The Pyromaniac is a Loud and Proud farter who has chosen to specialize in a specific field, a firm believer in the "blaze of glory" approach to life. The fire starter of the farting world, he will generally practice his art at parties, gathering all around him with the promise of great hilarity. When he is happy that he has a captive audience he will lay back, light up, and let rip.

Favored Fart: The Ripper or the Ripsnorter suits his antics well. However, any fart that will provide a suitable flame throwing experience is fine by the Pyromaniac.

Butthole Boffin

The scientist or geeky nerd, depending on your point of view, of the farting world. This strange specimen doesn't necessarily enjoy the act of farting itself, rather he has an almost obsessive interest in the sounds and smells generated by both his and other people's bottoms. Extreme cases will have notebooks filled with their observations and marks for all the best farts they have ever witnessed.

Favored Fart: A keen observer of all kinds of farts, but has an

Just when the handler needed his bottom as an added deterrent—it turned from blow to suck...

unhealthy interest in the gaseous emissions of other people's bottoms. Particularly interested in bizarre-sounding or smelling farts.

Ladies Who Launch:

Like the truth, they're out there somewhere. As has been observed earlier in the book, generally speaking the female of the species is far less likely to take pride in the product of her rectal ruminations than the male. There are, of course, some honorable exceptions to this rule and they can be gathered under the broad umbrella of Ladies Who Launch. Said ladies can be of any of the listed variety of farter but are distinct by virtue of their rarity value.

Favored Fart: Will depend on their chosen field of operation but it is a rare delight to find oneself in the presence of a Ripper-emitting Loud and Proud Lady Who's Launching.

Victorian etiquette demanded that society ladies should stand downwind of any floral display before eructing like the Clapham gasworks.

10–15, the average number of farts per day for a man. 8 or 9, the average number of farts per day for a woman. They do it less, but they do indeed do it on a regular basis.

In his autobiographical *Confessions*, French Enlightenment author Jean-Jacques Rousseau wrote of the Comtesse de Vercelles, "In the agonies of death, she broke wind loudly. 'Good!' she said, 'A woman who can fart is not dead!'"

After six glasses of light ale, the vicar's wife stunned the assembled company by challenging them to a who-can-fart-loudest competition.

> "Beans, beans are good for your heart. The more you eat the more you fart."
>
> Playground rhyme

When and Where

There are a number of occasions when a well-timed trump is the perfect accompaniment to the activity in which you are indulging. However, it's not always good to fart. On the whole it's a matter of timing and knowing when it is appropriate to let it all out. In the following paragraphs I shall attempt to give a brief guide to when and where you should and shouldn't give free reign to your rectal repertoire.

"What winde can there blow, that doth not some men please? A fart in the blowing doth the blower ease."

John Heyward

As Claire struggled to choose between her lover and her husband, an unexpectedly loud Ripsnorter further strained the atmosphere.

In the Bath

The poor man's Jacuzzi. Just sit back, relax (but not too much—bubbles good, floaters bad), and let go to your heart's content. With enough practice and suitable muscle control, you will be able to create a bubbling symphony all of your own, the farter's bathtime equivalent of new age mood music. It should be noted that this may not be such a good idea if you are sharing a bath. It would be wise to ascertain the other person's views before you impress them with your "home spa" technique.

Marilyn blasted out the chorus to I'm Forever Blowing Bubbles.

"If a man knows not what harbor he seeks, any wind is the right wind."

Seneca

At Sporting Events (as a member of the crowd)

A sporting event can provide the ideal opportunity for a variety of farting exploits. If a spot of undercover public farting is what you're after, then the noise of the crowd and the assorted smells of large numbers of sweaty people and junk food crammed into the kind of close proximity that would shame a battery farm, will mask all but the most strident and stinking of bottom burps.

Imagine yourself at a football match in the middle of the massed throng just as your team have scored. Everyone is jumping up and down in blissful rapture, shouting and screaming their appreciation. You will never have a better chance to let fly with real grade-A Ripsnorter undetected. A truly joyous occasion for the Sly and Retiring farter as they can give full vent to their bowels and remain completely anonymous.

Alternatively, if you are a Loud and Proud farter and are unfortunate enough to be witnessing a truly dire performance by the team or player of your choice, you may well consider that passing comment by passing wind is the best way to let both the culprit and the rest of the crowd

Only two people in the grandstand knew why the 100m sprint was plagued with false starts...

know of your disappointment. Always wait for a suitably quiet lull in crowd participation if this is your aim.

"What comfort can the vortices of Descartes give to a man who has whirlwinds in his bowels."

Benjamin Franklin

This time Helga let go too early, with devastating results for her style marks.

Ski Jumping

As with many things in life, when you are a ski jumper, an extra few inches can make all the difference between success and failure. If you can maintain a constant stream of farts as you ski down the slope toward the jump, you will not only increase your velocity but you'll also lose a little body weight. Ideally, you will be able to save an exceptional Ripper for the exact point of takeoff, thrusting you into the air with all the power available of turbo trumping.

SATAN

Meeting Royalty

Now this may seem like a strange choice to have in the "Where To" section but consider what royalty actually do for a living. Royals spend a large amount of their time meeting people that they have absolutely nothing in common with and about whom they know only what their advisers have told them minutes beforehand. Despite these handicaps they always manage to come across as interested, polite people—it's what they do. Now with this in mind, if you are in line waiting to meet a royal and you want to fart, hold on and wait for them to get level with you. Drop your curtsy or bow and drop your guts—it will be an educational experience finding out how they choose to smooth over the event and make polite conversation in the wake of your bottom concerto. Who knows? You may even be able to pick up a few tips on how to excuse yourself in future farting escapades.

Edward VII was once riding in a state carriage with the Kaiser (Wilhelm II of Germany), his nephew. They heartily disliked each other but had to keep up a show of friendly conversation. Suddenly one of the horses committed a misdemeanor, which unpleasantly contaminated the air of the carriage. Both monarchs ignored it, then it

It was a hanging offense to fart in front of the king...but, thankfully, the king usually farted first.

happened again and King Edward, as host, felt forced to apologize for the smell. "My dear uncle Bertie," the Kaiser replied, "please don't mention it—I really thought it was one of the horses."

"In doleful Scenes, that
breaks our heart,
Punch comes, like you,
and lets a Fart."

Jonathon Swift, *Mad Mullinix and Timothy*

"The Queen of France just
touched this Globe.
And the Pestilence
darted from her robe."

William Blake, *Lafayette*

"Son, both you know and I know it wasn't the hoss."

1,250,000—number of web sites found when the word "fart" is entered in a search engine; popular subject farting!

Where Not To Fart

Weddings and Funerals

It's always going to be seen as bad form to drop your guts at a formal religious service, especially if you're the minister. If you do happen to let one slip out at a funeral it would pay to be near the casket—you may get away with it if people assume that the smell emanating from your bottom is actually coming from the corpse. This is a situation in which silence is not so much golden as absolutely essential.

Of course if you truly detest the person being buried or married and you don't care what everyone else thinks, you may consider that a well-timed Ripsnorter is the perfect send-off.

> If I'm in a restaurant and someone asks, "Do you mind if I smoke?" I always say, "No, do you mind if I fart?"
>
> Steve Martin, American comedian

Jim's request of "pull my finger" was considered bad etiquette for a black-tie dinner.

Meeting his girlfriends' parents was always going to be difficult situation, but at the last moment Nigel's bottom went critical...

Meet the Parents

Meeting the parents of your new love is always a nerve-racking experience. It can only be made more so if your behind chooses this particular time to misbehave—unless the father turns out to be a Loud and Proud farter. In this case take him aside for a man-to-man chat and let it all out. (Remember his greatest fear is that you will replace him as the alpha farter in the household.)

Should you find yourself sitting around the dinner table and unable to contain the eruptions in your pants, then you have a couple of choices. Firstly, you could try and lay the blame elsewhere. Always go for the pet, *never* another member of the family. This can work well if you only let one or two farts out and they are not so loud that they can be instantly traced to your ass. However this line of attack is fraught with danger as the following story demonstrates. This tale may well be apocryphal but it serves as a suitable warning.

A young man is dining for the first time with his girlfriend's parents. All is going well until unable to contain himself any longer he squeezes out a real stinker. The father lifts the tablecloth and shouts down at the family dog: "Rover, get out!"

Mightily relieved, in more ways than one, the young man relaxes. The meal continues to go well until, a short while later the young man drops his guard and another hummer emerges. Again the father shouts: "Rover, get out!"

Thinking that he has got away with it, the young man decides that he may as well let loose everything he's got, leaving himself free to enjoy the rest of the evening. With this in mind he carefully eases out his remaining gas. As before the father lifts the tablecloth and shouts at the dog again: "Rover, get out before he gasses you to death." Our hero is shamefaced and never invited back.

If there is no family pet or you feel that you dare not risk the above scenario, the only advice I can offer is to act suitably embarrassed, apologize profusely, and claim a rare medical condition that has the doctors baffled but which you are assiduously seeking treatment for. The sympathy vote may save the day for you.

"Oh son, I believe you. You're not a farter, no, and Hiram here isn't the cutest bitty plaything since Art Garfunkel."

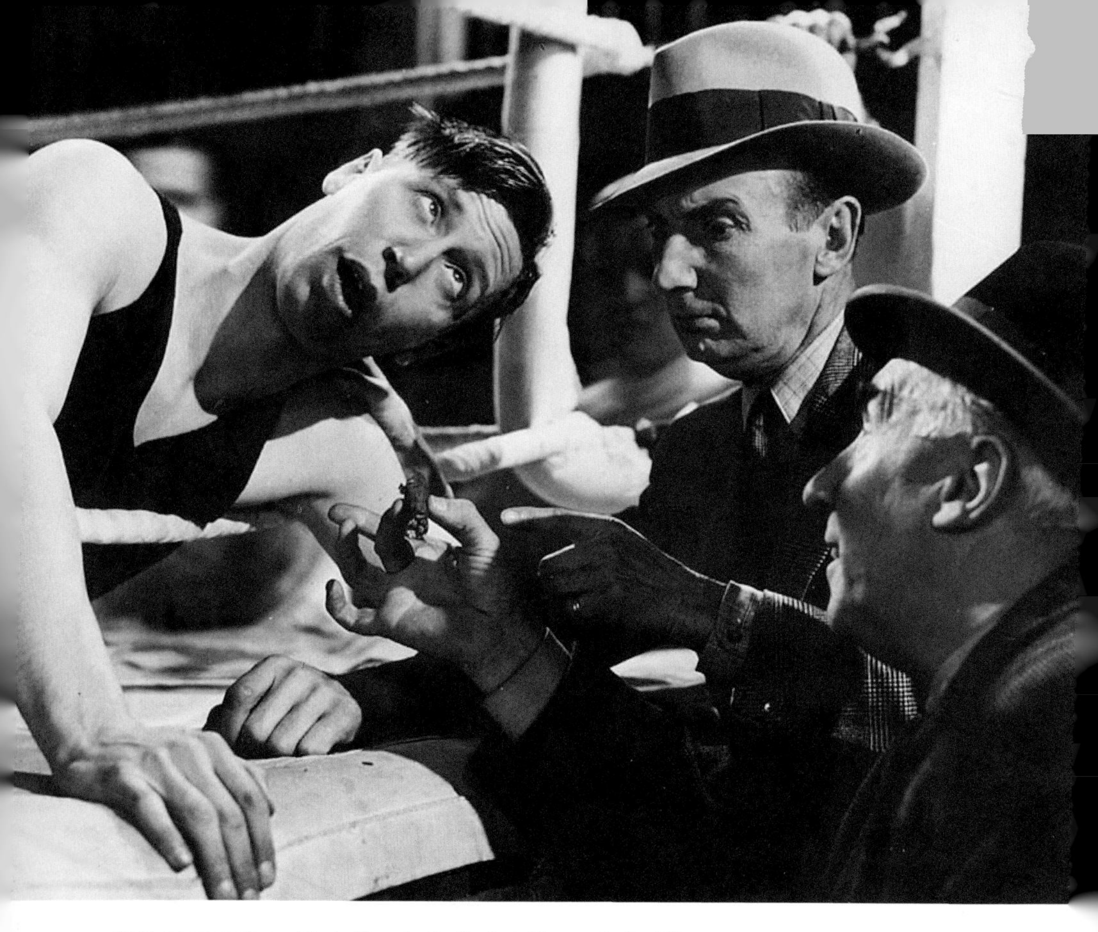

"Kid, we warned you. Floats like a butterfly, farts like an elephant."

At Sporting Events (as a participant)

Picture the scene: it's the final game of the World Pool Championships, the drama being played out before a packed auditorium. It all hangs on the shot you're about to take. Glory or failure, it could go either way—make the shot and you're a hero, miss it and no one will even remember that you were there. You circle the table, weighing up your options, measuring the angles until you finally decide on exactly which shot and how to play it. As the tension mounts you chalk the cue, blow off the excess dust, and stroll to the table to prepare to take your shot at glory. Just as you bend over your nerves get the better of you and an enormous fart erupts from your behind, ringing out around the hushed auditorium. Let's face it, you're going to miss the shot but everyone is going to remember that you were there (for all the wrong reasons as far as you're concerned).

I would love to see the day when an umpire at Wimbledon farts so violently that he or she topples off their precarious-looking high chair. Great comedy value for the audience but probably a career-ending move for the umpire, and one that could well lead to serious physical injury and years spent on the therapist's couch.

On Trial

While it may be true that the law is an ass, exercising yours in court could land you in serious trouble. Judges will not take kindly to flatulence in their courtrooms. The English phrase "up before the beak" came about due to the almost unnaturally sensitive nature of the judiciary's nasal passages, these guys can sniff out a Ripsnorter at a hundred paces—and they are not impressed. If you're in the dock attempting to plead your innocence of all the nefarious charges leveled against you, you're not going to help your cause if you can't control your bottom. Prosecuting counsel will always be tempted to advise a jury that such obvious signs of nervousness can only point to a guilty conscience. Yes, they can smell something funny all right.

Members of the jury be warned, you too are not exempt from the wrath of the gowned and gavel-wielding ladies and gentlemen in the top seat. However if you wish to cut short your spell of jury service and are prepared to pay a couple of fines, your bottom could serve you well. If you can maintain a constant stream of first degree stinkers, the judge will most probably evict you and your offending rear end from their courtroom.

Though he had spent all morning talking out of it, it was a spontaneous burst from the defense lawyer that most gripped the court's attention.

Brigadier Ponsonby-Smith gave a new meaning to the phrase "friendly fire."

Business Meetings

There you stand in the boardroom putting forward your fantastic new proposal, the one that's guaranteed to take your career to stratospheric new heights. You've got the directors and your potential new clients eating out of the palm of your hand and things just couldn't be going better. A faint twitching in your back passage sets the alarm bells ringing, you know you've got something brewing but you know there's no way you can let it out now.

You can't afford to rush through the rest of your presentation because you really need to clinch this deal. Straining to contain yourself, you manfully continue to make your pitch. Finally, near the end and casting your gaze around the room, you are confident of success. Just as you finish your closing arguments, you relax for a fatal split second and a fart of gargantuan proportions erupts from your pants. All your good work, not to mention your lucky underwear, is wasted. You will not be remembered as the high flyer who grasped his opportunity, but rather as the young pretender who literally and metaphorically blew it when he had the chance. In high pressure business situations like this let your motto be "clench to clinch."

In Space

Some things are a cliché just because they are self-evidently true, hence the expression, "About as welcome as a fart in a space suit." If you think about it, stuck in a space suit is about the worst place you can be if you have just dropped a real stinker. It's the most enclosed space you could possibly find yourself in; there really isn't anywhere to run to in order to get away from the masochistic stench you have inflicted upon yourself. Worse still is the fact that it will circulate around the suit for some time, revisiting your nostrils again and again. Even when it's finally died off the suit won't exactly feel "lemon fresh."

But quite possibly the worst nightmare of a farter would be to follow through in the middle of a space walk. Just imagine the horror, not to say shame, of gazing out on the panoramic vista of infinite space while in the confined company of your own free-floating floaters.

The mission was to study solar winds. But right now Astronaut 29067 Schumacher was studying winds much closer to home.

Flying Lesson

You really can't afford to let rip during a your first flying lesson in a small airplane. Let's face it, you won't be able to pilot the plane and if it's enough of a stinker it could well endanger your life, as the guy who does know how to fly the thing struggles with his nose rather than with the controls. What you want is to feel the wind beneath your wings as you glide gracefully through the thermal currents. What you don't want is to feel the wind in your pants as you hurtle toward the ground at an alarming rate of knots.

"For gentle wind does move, silently invisible."

William Blake

As the ground grew ever closer, Al wished he'd left his ass back in the hangar.

“Leuca in presence
once a fart did let
Some laughed a little;
she forsook the place
And, mad with shame,
did her glove forget
Which she returned to
fetch with bashful grace
And when she should have said,
“This is my glove,”
“My fart,” quoth she, which did
more laughter move.”

Sir John Davies, *In Lucucam*

"You'll no get away wi' it laddy; this here's a non-farting bar. Now move ya coat slowly to the door..."

"My Lord, we have quite forgot the fart."

Queen Elizabeth 1 to Edward de Vere, Earl of Oxford, who went into self-imposed exile for several years after farting loudly in court while bowing before his queen.

Farting In History

Man and beast have been happily farting since life first emerged from the primordial soup. It is one of the few activities that provide a common link from ancient times through to the present and beyond. Shamefully, academics have wilfully neglected to place farting in its proper historical context. Some measure of recompense can now be offered as we examine just a few of the key events in the history of the world that were in fact shaped by the farts and farters of their times.

> "All citizens shall be allowed to pass gas whenever necessary."
>
> Claudius Caesar

1925: Bertie shows Helen the true meaning of the word "flapper."

Elizabeth 1 suffered from chronic wind. Here, in an early photo, we see the "virgin queen" lifting one royal ass cheek to allow good circulation around court.

The Great Fire of London

On September 2, 1666, the city of London was destroyed by fire. An area one and a half miles by half a mile, containing 87 churches and 13,200 houses was consumed in the blaze. It has long been claimed that the fire was started in the house and shop of King Charles II's baker, Thomas Farynor. Farynor forgot to put out the fire in his oven when he retired for the night causing the embers to ignite a stack of firewood close by.

While this version is, in the main, the true sequence of events, it misses out a large and highly relevant part of the tale. The diaries of one Corben Pumper, a successful merchant who lived on the outskirts of the city, reveal the more likely cause of the fire. Pumper's diaries make frequent reference to his membership of "Ye Merrie Clubbe of Gentlemen Farters." It is well known that taking snuff in order to induce a sneezing fit was a popular pastime in England at this time. What is less well documented is the number of social clubs similar to Pumper's who would gather together to "practice the noble arte of flatulence in the company of like-minded gentlemen and away from the pinched faces and scolding expressions of the fairer sex." The entry in Pumper's diary dated September 1, 1666, gives some clue to the true course of events the following night...

"Against my better judgement we have admitted to the ranks of the Clubbe the Royal baker, one Thomas Farynor. He seems a common sort to me but the vote was in his favor as he has connections of some note and has promised a fine finale to our next meeting. As is our custom on admitting a new member the next gathering shall be at his abode.

Tomorrow I shall eat well my fill of beans and pulses and in the night we shall gather at his bakery and break wind in common throughout the night. Farynor has been tight-lipped about the finale he has planned but my good friend Dr. Rathbone who proposed him has whispered to me that the baker will attempt to impress us with a trick he calls 'the flame from within.' Though I am distrustful of the baker I would have to admit that I am intrigued by the prospect of this finale."

Pumper, Rathbone, and their fellow farters did indeed spend a sociable night farting away to their heart's content. At the end of their gaseous night Farynor let rip a real beauty and lit his fart with disastrous consequences. It is surely due to a guilty conscience that after this date Pumper makes no further reference in his diaries to his beloved clubbe.

The creature had borne a fair resemblance to Justin Timberlake before the doctor's evil experiments to create his trumping tyrant, "The Gasman."

His dragon breath was bad enough, but when Godzilla let one rip, Tokyo would disappear into the sea.

Extinction of the Dinosaurs

In their quest to deny farting its rightful place in the history of our planet, boffins have come up with a number of theories to explain the extinction of the dinosaurs. The most popular is that a giant meteor hit the planet causing various drastic climactic changes. Nonsense!

There were an awful lot of very large and entirely vegetarian dinosaurs. Have you ever been in a room with a large vegetarian? These guys can fart to Olympic standards, their behinds are such Weapons of Mass Eruction you want to chew your own nose off to escape the smell.

Carnivorous dinosaurs would by nature have attacked their herbivore cousins. The herbivores would naturally fight back with all available force. In many cases their sheer size would have been enough to see off the predators, however if this failed they would have had to develop alternative self-defense mechanisms. Is it so ridiculous to believe that by turning their back on their attacker and firing one off from the vast fart factory in their behind they could stun him with both the force and the smell of the ensuing fart? This would of course provide the opportunity to either flee, or kill their opponent while he was down.

As the battles between carnivores and herbivores escalated, the level of dinosaur farting would have increased. At some point the amount of dinosaur fart gas in the atmosphere would have reached critical mass and begun to kill off both dinosaurs and plant life, leaving carnivores and herbivores fighting over an ever-decreasing food supply. In a nutshell, the dinosaurs farted themselves to death.

Discovery of the Theory of Gravity

Legend has it that Sir Isaac Newton was leaning against a tree quietly minding his own business when an apple fell on his head. This chance event led to the formulation of his theory of gravity, that what goes up must come down.

Once again that which is recorded is lacking in vital detail. While scientists are keen to tell us about the intellectual leap of imagination which led Newton to this understanding of the world, they are less eager to point out exactly how it happened. The, until now, unrecorded reason for the apple's fall was the vast Ripper which the learned gentleman had just unleashed from his hose. The vibrations from which had traveled directly from his bottom, up the trunk of the tree, and loosened the apple as it dangled precariously above his head.

Who knows how long mankind would have had to wait for this cornerstone of scientific theory if it had not been for the timely trump that Sir Isaac unleashed.

Signor Cavallino soon found out it was not just cowboys who gorged themselves on beans before taking to the saddle.

...one loud parp later and the The Doc lay dying. Hank was confused. Those stories he'd believed all those years—they were plain wrong. He who smelt it hadn't dealt it...

Gunfight at the OK Corral

In the Wild West town of Tombstone, trouble had been brewing between the Earp brothers and a gang known as the Cowboys for some time. Accounts of what exactly happened are mixed but what is agreed on is that it all culminated in a gunfight outside the OK Corral.

As the two parties squared up to each other, they were faced with the classic Mexican stand-off, just without any actual Mexicans. Trigger fingers twitching, the gunfighters eyed each other up, all parties waiting for the first move to be made. A shot rang out and all hell let loose in a hail of lead which lasted for only thirty seconds but which left three of the Cowboys dead and nearly all parties injured.

The sad truth is that the whole sorry scene could have been avoided and a peaceful solution found if it had not been for the nervous eruption from one of the participant's pants. For you see that fatal first shot was not fired from a pistol but rather from the rear end of an unnamed, but skittish gunslinger.

History teaches us many lessons in life. You have been warned. An injudicious fart can have serious consequences. It really is all about knowing when, where, and how.

Flight

On June 4, 1783, the Montgolfier brothers, Joseph and Etienne, thrilled the French population of Annonay with the first public demonstration of their hot-air balloon. Like many men before him Joseph had often looked up to the sky and seen the clouds floating serenely in the air and wondered what it would be like to be up there among them, looking down on the world below.

One day while reclining on a chaise longue and dreaming his dreams, Joseph had a revelation. As his mind pondered the seeming impossibility of his vision his bottom provided him with the answer to his problem. At the time Joseph was wearing a pair of pantaloons with a back-fastening flap, as was the fashion of the time. Upon letting rip a real corker of a fart, Joseph, having forgotten to button up his rear flap, noticed that it was lifted into the air by the result of his exertions.

Joseph shared his discovery with his brother and Etienne's imagination was similarly inspired. There followed many experiments as the brothers attempted to discover the key element in making the rising gas. A constant diet of beans and pulses followed, with much wearing of unfastened pantaloons. At first the brothers were misled by

With vapor trailing from the cockpit, spectators below thought Carl's impending crash was a display stunt and cheered the avaitor all the way down.

the fact that their greatest successes seemed to occur when their farts were at their smelliest. It took a number of weeks and no small amount of gagging before Joseph and Etienne realized that the smell was mere coincidence and that it was actually the hot air that they were emitting that was causing their pantaloon flaps to rise with such force.

There were also a fair number of singed eyebrows and scorched pantaloons when Joseph and Etienne finally realized that by lighting their farts even greater results could be achieved.

Having achieved great success with their bottoms the brothers moved on from their pantaloon-related experiments. They realized early on that they would never be able to generate the required amount of hot air from their derrieres to make manned flight possible. Instead they calculated the size of animal required to generate such an amount, but found that it would weigh too much to make the experiment feasible (although a hot-air balloon powered by up-turned farting elephants is an amusing image). Finally the brothers Montgolfier turned to more conventional methods of experimentation which eventually led to their successful demonstration at Annonay.

Once again the part of the fart in a great moment of history has been completely wiped from the records.

Stop Press: Scientists have just discovered methane on Mars. Proof that if there are alien life forms, they too enjoy a good fart. Farting is thus proved to be a universal pursuit and we can look forward to comparing notes with our intergalactic cousins. One can only hope that the narrow-minded boffins see fit to include a copy of this book in all future pods launched into space in an attempt to contact aliens and explain our society to them.

"Chevy Chase couldn't ad lib a fart after a baked-bean dinner."

Johnny Carson, American chat show host

England rugby captain Will Carling famously described the English Rugby Union committee as "57 old farts." He was immediately replaced as captain.

George could never understand why there was no man in Gloria's life. Twenty-five seconds into their first knee-trembler, he could.

"A man may break a word with you sir; and words are but wind; Ay, and break it in your face."

William Shakespeare, *A Comedy of Errors*

The Path of the Third Eye

There are many who enjoy the worthy art of flatulence, but few are they who can truly claim to have mastered the dark art. There exists a sacred band of dedicated farters known as the followers of the Path of the Third Eye who recognize each other through various secret signals. These can range from trouser legs inflated in a specific fashion and certain secret farts that only the initiated will be able to perform and recognize.

Very little of substance is known of the internal workings of this worthy order. The following information is based upon some ancient manuscripts that were anonymously posted to the author.

It is pointless to seek out the brotherhood for if they deem you to be worthy they shall find you and offer to train you in the Art of the Fart. Should you wish to advertise your dedication to the cause of flatulence, you should simply ensure that you take every opportunity to publicly proclaim your intentions and fart as often and as well as you can in any and all social situations. Be warned, however, that the path to enlightenment is a long and arduous trail. Many are those who have tried and been found wanting.

You too can master a face like this if you study the divine Path of the Third Eye. Though hemorrhoids has a similar effect.

If you can answer yes to all of the following questions then you may have what it takes to embark on this most fulfilling of quests:

1. Do you actively enjoy a good fart? ☐

2. Are you prepared to risk all dignity in the pursuit of farting excellence? ☐

3. Have you eaten specific meals with a view to achieving a truly great farting experience? ☐

4. Are you always ready to give due acknowledgment to the farting excellence of others? ☐

Mrs Snape was forever encouraging Quentin to try farting an octave higher. "Clench and eruct like this..."

"...I had got some cold, and so in pain by wind. A sure precursor of pain is a sudden letting of farts. And when that stops, then my passages stop and my pain begins."

Samuel Pepys' diary entry,
June 20th, 1664

If you are fortunate enough to be sought out by the brothers you will be expected to cast aside all worldly concerns and concentrate fully on your training at one of their secret hideaways. There will be various stages of expertise that you must achieve and at each stage you will be expected to complete a range of feats and tests known as The Rites of the Passage. Only when mastery of all rites is achieved may you continue to the next level of training.

There now follows a brief guide to the four ranks of farting that you can move through and the trials you will undergo.

A true brother will not shirk from his coaching duties even at formal occasions. Here a Grand Master advises on the best choice for wind generation from the table d'hôte.

For ten minutes neither man spoke, both knowing the unwritten rule, he who supplied it, denied it.

"Acting is largely a matter of farting about in disguises."

Peter O'Toole, British actor

"I have more talent in my smallest fart than you have in your entire body."

Walter Matthau to Barbra Streisand

"The wind in a man's face makes him wise."

S. Palmer, *Moral Essays On Proverbs*

The Apprentice Farter

Brown Eye

Thus named as it is written, "He who strains too hard for perfection in the early stages may suffer the dreaded follow through."

When first you are accepted into the hallowed ranks to begin your rear-end ruminations, you will live in a small, unventilated room for one month. For this month, you will exist solely on a diet of baked beans, curry, cabbage, and carbonated drinks (no product placement here, they're all equally good in farting terms). This is a toughening-up process during which you will learn to live with all the most noxious smells that you can create. More importantly, you will find your true inner voice and the farts at which you excel (mastery of all styles of fart is available to only the most naturally gifted of followers).

At the completion of your month of solitary contemplation you will commence a program of yogic exercises aimed at producing above-average muscular control.

When your masters believe that you have progressed suitably, you will be sent back out into the world to attempt your first Rites of The Passage. At this stage you will be asked to demonstrate the basic lack of

With most people, champagne went straight to their head; but for Hubert it had completely the opposite effect.

public shame in your farting, the ability to fart on command, and volume and odor capacity above the norm. Remember not all candidates are successful at their first attempt—if at first you don't succeed, fart, fart, and fart again.

Brown Eye Rites of the Passage

• We can all fart loudly enough to wake ourselves up (come on, you've all done it). To demonstrate your progress, you must be able to fart loudly enough to wake both yourself and your partner and the smell should be sufficient to induce minor gagging in your partner. You will be expected to show no nasal after-effects whatsoever.

• You will be taken to a library and instructed to unleash a tirade of your chosen farts. These should be of sufficient volume to disturb all readers in the reference section (smell is not judged at this stage) and eventually lead to you being evicted by at least two irate librarians. At no time should you show any signs of embarrassment—any reddening of the cheeks (we're talking face here) will lead to failure and the need to re-take the test.

• Upon successful completion of these trials, you will be officially declared a Brown Eye and will progress to further training.

"When you said you were going to keep the bed warm, I was expecting a hot water bottle!"

"The duke shew'd me all his fine house; and the duchess. From her closet brought out a full purse in all her clutches. I talked of a peace, and they both gave a start, His Grace swore by God, and Her Grace let a fart."

Jonathon Swift, *An Excellent New Song*

"I should like one of these days to be so well known, so popular, so celebrated, so famous, that it would permit me… to break wind in society and society would think it a most natural thing."

Honore De Balzac, French novelist

Purple Eye

Thus named as it is written, "He who overstretches his own boundaries before mastery is achieved may well find himself bruised in private places."

When you return to your training both your diet and exercise regime will move to the next level. Chilies, raw onions, hot dogs, and beer will be added to your menu. No salve will be supplied and if any is found about your person you will be summarily dismissed from the order—you must continue to toughen up for the challenges that lie ahead. Far greater muscular control must be achieved and you will be expected to begin mastering all styles of fart, not simply your own party tricks. Just as sumo wrestlers are trained to tuck their private parts away to keep them from danger at critical moments, thus you will learn to keep your wind at bay until the appropriate moment, at which point you will be able to release as much or as little in a style of your own choosing.

You must demonstrate improved control and the ability to generate a truly obnoxious stench at will.

Edmund faces the outrage caused by a well-timed Ripsnorter with the cool nonchalance of a Purple Eye farter...while checking on his stock prices.

After the will was read, young master Sidney celebrated getting the house, the estate, and most important of all, the 217 books of fart gags.

Purple Eye Rites of the Passage

- Not only must you be able to wake yourself and anyone sharing your bed up, you must now be able to set your rear end to go off at a specific time, acting as an alarm clock. You will be given a different time for each day of a full week and be expected to rumble and rise to order.

- You will return to the library, in disguise as librarians have long memories, where you must proceed to stroll nonchalantly around and emit a series of Silent But Violent farts of such magnitude that the entire library is emptied before you are identified as the culprit.

- Back at the training hideaway you will be put through your paces in a time trial during which you must provide to order a specific range of farts chosen by your trainer. These must end on a double-barreled fart containing no fewer than seven syllables.

Upon successful completion of these trials you will be officially declared a Purple Eye and will progress to further training.

Master of Farts

Black Eye

Thus named as it is written, "While striving toward the darker, more public, practices many trials will be failed by all but the most adept of students. Such public failure will meet with swift rebuke and most likely a poke in the eye."

Very few have the capacity to progress to the level of Master of Farts. True dedication is required as, at this level, you will be expected to master not only your own bottom but also begin to know the specific movements of those around you. You will nurture the ability to recognize the sounds and smells generated by other farters.

As your yoga training progresses, you must master the art of ventriloquist farting, the ability to "throw" your farts so that they appear to have come from someone else's bottom.

With a limited budget for the big finale, the cast of The Gathering Storm *were forced to improvise...*

With consumate ease Constable Arbuthnot "threw" a Ripper into the station officer's earpiece

Black Eye Rites of the Passage

• Once more to the library and a chance of revenge for your earlier eviction. Disguised once more, you must take your seat in the library and proceed to "throw" a series of gargantuan Rippers that will sound as if they are being let off by the librarian. You must continue in this vein until, despite his self-righteous protestations, either his manager or irate members of the public forcibly remove the librarian. Be warned—it is frowned upon to return repeatedly and attempt to have the librarian fired for continuous farting. Not only must you exercise restraint at all times but in this case you have one more humiliation in store for him/her.

• At a hideaway, you will be blindfolded and led into a room full of your contemporaries where you will be tested in a game of Blind Man's Guff. Your fellow pupils will take it in turns to let rip an assortment of farts and you must be able to identify the purveyor of each fart by either sound or smell.

• Upon successful completion of these trials, you will be officially declared a Black Eye and will progress to further training.

Grand Master of Farts

White Eye

Thus named as it is written "The true master of the Art of the Fart will maintain, throughout all his rear-end ruminations, a gleaming, pristine third eye for he has full mastery of his every movement."

To achieve Grand Master status you must be able to attain an almost Zen-like level of control over your bowels. Full mastery of ventriloquist farting will be required, the ability to "throw" both the sound and the smell of your farts. No food or drink that does not increase your farting capacity may pass your lips, for your body has now become a temple to trumping—you live to launch.

> "It's an ill wind that blows no good."
>
> Proverb

A double bubble bath work-out was always going to be a risky proposition when you had a Grand Master training with a less experienced Brown Eye.

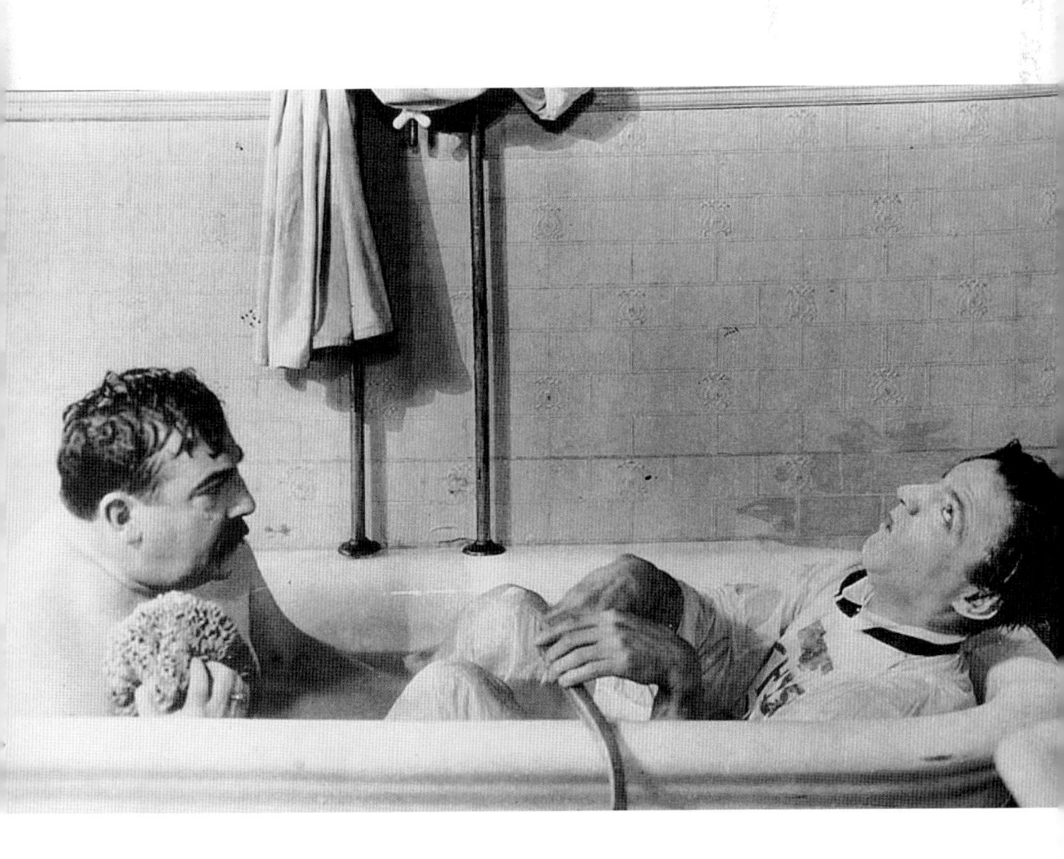

White Eye Rites of the Passage

There remain but two tests you must pass (including the final act of humiliation for our friend the librarian).

- An advanced level of Blind Man's Guff will be performed. You must go to a bar and be able to locate the purveyor of every fart and be able to distinguish exactly what meal was eaten to provide the smell.

- To the library one last time. You must be strong of purpose and stomach, for today you shall demonstrate awesome, not to say vindictive, powers. Take your seat, sit back, relax, and "throw" a wet fart into the pants of the librarian. As his surprise and discomfort become obvious you may now reveal your identity to him as there is nothing he can do.

Upon successful completion of these trials you will be officially declared a White Eye and sent out into the world to search for future Grand Masters.

"Another bottle? Don't worry honey, I know how to attract the waiter's attention..."

“Klopstock felt the intripled turn
And all his bowels began to churn
And his bowels turned
round three times three
And lockd in his soul
with a ninefold key
That from his body it
neer could be parted
Till to the last trumpet
it was farted”

William Blake, *When Klopstock England Denied*

Their marriage was in tatters. It wasn't a question of keeping it up any more; it was a question of keeping the bedclothes from imitating an inflatable tennis court.

"Not I, not I, but the wind that blows through me"

D.H. Lawrence, *Song Of A Man Who Has Come Through*

Real Life Farting Heroes #1: Le Petomane

Joseph Pujol, better known as Le Petomane, was a French entertainer who was popular in the Parisian music halls in the late nineteenth century. He was the first artiste in Western history to earn his living from farting. Now that's something to aspire to—being paid to parp.

Pujol was born in Marseilles on June 1, 1857. It was while swimming at the beach as a child that he first noticed something unusual. When he was swimming in the sea, he felt something cold seeping into his stomach. When he ran back onto the beach, he felt water pouring out of his rear end. It was in later life, when he was telling this story to some comrades in the army, that Pujol was encouraged to try and repeat the experience. It was only then that he realized that he had a "special gift."

Returning to the beach he found that with suitable contraction of his bowel muscles he could suck as much water as he wanted into his back passage and then expel it at will. Pujol was soon the life and soul of his barracks as he entertained his fellow soldiers with his back passage blow-out antics. He also found that by holding his breath he could suck air into his bowels and force it out in a controlled fashion.

Herman knew that the Führer was truly evil when he stopped to enjoy the rising odor from his signature fart, the Sauerkraut surprise.

When he left the army, Pujol returned to the bakery he had opened in Marseilles and carried on using his gift to entertain his friends and customers. You just don't get service like that in the stores these days!

"...And if you're going to do the national anthem, I want it coming out of your mouth not your ass."

A local promoter got wind of Pujol's performances and convinced him to try his luck in a more public arena. The promoter hired a hall and advertised the upcoming event all over the town. It was at this time that Pujol chose his stage name of Le Petomane (the farting man). It didn't take long for the popularity of Le Petomane's antics to reach such heights that advertising was no longer necessary—his shows sold out every night.

In 1892, after touring his act around the provinces, Pujol felt the time was right to achieve his long-held ambition to take his show to the world-renowned Moulin Rouge in Paris. Le Petomane entertained his audience by releasing a series of farts which he gave names to; The Little Girl, The Mother-in-Law, The Bride on her Wedding Night (a very quiet fart), The Bride the Morning After (a very loud fart), The Mason, and his *piece de resistance*—a ten-second Ripper called The Dressmaker, Tearing Two Yards of Calico. He would then go backstage and return with a rubber tube that he inserted into his anus and proceeded to "smoke" a cigarette. This was followed by rear-end flute playing, the blowing out of a number of flames, and all topped off by inviting his audience to sing along with him. Pujol's act was so successful that it took him all over Europe. At one point, though, he so outraged the great and good of Madrid that he was forced to see out his tenure there as a mere clown, with no farting whatsoever.

Now there was a guy who really knew how to make the most of his ass(ets).

Real Life Farting Heroes #2: Mr. Methane

Inheriting the farting mantle of Le Petomane is the modern-day fart showman, Mr. Methane. Dressed in a bright green leotard and cape, Mr. Methane looks like a farting superhero. In the words of one of his fans, the actor Kelsey Grammer, "This man took the history books by the pages and really ripped one out for himself!"

Fortunately for the rest of us, Mr. Methane doesn't just rip one out for himself, he does so in public for our entertainment. He presents an eruction-filled stage show which combines various forms of modern and classical music, accompanied by acts such as the rear-end trumpet, the snuffing out of candles, the blowing out of talcum powder, and dart farting.

The gentlemen were impressed by the lady's typing skills, appearance, and good manners, but mostly by her ability to produce the sound of a bazooka when required.

Standing downwind of Captain Montgomery was always an unpleasant experience for any nearby colleagues.

"Jerry Ford is so dumb that he can't fart and chew gum at the same time."

Lyndon B. Johnson referring to President Gerald Ford

"Bacteria in the large intestine produce the accumulation of gas that causes flatulence. When these bugs consume certain types of carbohydrates, called oligosaccharides, they produce a mix of gases that includes methane and certain sulphur-containing gases. On average, adults produce four to five litres of gas a day, and beans are the vegetables most commonly associated with excess wind. That is because up to 60 per cent of their carbohydrates are oligosaccharides. "

Percy Bysshe Shelley

Top Tens: Songs

1.	Blowing In The Wind – Bob Dylan
2.	Burning From The Inside – Bauhaus
3.	Oops I Did It Again – Britney Spears
4.	Brown Eyed Girl – Van Morrison
5.	Good Vibrations – Beach Boys
6.	The Parps of Peace – Paul McCartney
7.	She's Like The Wind – Patrick Swayze
8.	I Feel the Earth Move – Carole King
9.	Wind Beneath My Wings – Bette Midler
10.	Ring of Fire – Johnny Cash

"Young lady! Any more of that and you'll be blowing yourself all the way back to Kansas again!"

Books

1.	Fart From the Madding Crowd - Thomas Hardy
2.	Wind In The Willows - Kenneth Grahame
3.	Animal Fart - George Orwell
4.	Blast From The Past - Ben Elton
5.	Stinker, Tailor, Soldier, Spy - John Le Carré
6.	The Color Parp-le - Alice Walker
7.	Lord of the Rings - J.R.R. Tolkien
8.	Back Passage to India - E.M. Forster
9.	Trump - Donald Trump
10.	Delta of Anus - Anus Nin

With one expert squeeze, Grand Master Melvin (left) convinced his friends they were being attacked by a gang of revolver-wielding fiends.

Films

1.	Back Draft
2.	Blown Away
3.	Gone With The Wind
4.	The Great Escape
5.	A Shot In The Dark
6.	Fanny By Gaslight
7.	Blowup
8.	Rear Wind-ow
9.	The One That Got Away
10.	A Mighty Wind

"Happy birthday, Mr President!"

Contents of the Average Fart

59% nitrogen

21% hydrogen

9% carbon dioxide

7% methane

4% oxygen

None of the above contents actually smell. Less than 1% of the fart is made-up of the actual stench-inducing chemicals such as ammonia, hydrogen sulphide, and skatole.

"When you said you were loud in bed, this wasn't quite what I was expecting..."

"Mister, I can tear two yards of calico, imitate a ship in fog, and sound the five o'clock hooter; but if you think I'm blowing smoke rings with that cigar butt, you can whistle Dixie."